Opening Our Minds

Since when did Science have all the Answers about the creation of life ?
Well its Obvious they do not, but we will take a look into the Scientific theories surrounding life in it self.

Whats known about the unknown ? More specifically Sasquatch other known as Bigfoot , To some the impossible or a Camp fire story created as folklore.
Answers: Who has them ? No one but Who wants them well yeah we all do Right ?

In This book I clearly share blunt outspoken truth that many will still fail to understand or acknowledge when it comes to the proof of Sasquatch or the so called facts that so many address regarding our Cryptid friend, and yes I will address Sasquatch in this book as our Cryptid friend until reasons not to come to my attention.

The many Facts spoken by wanna be Researchers and enthusiast are all lies , Yes you heard me lies.
How do I know that they are Lies ? Well when we have speculation on an undiscovered species and you preach to the people stating that the assumptions are true not having nor providing solid proof to support your claim and so bluntly insisting to ignore your statements of being no more than speculation then its a lie created by a liar.

I want you to read this book carefully and here is Why; I have often made claims in my past based off the interest and love of this topic rather than having proof to support what I laid out there, and through the years I have come to correct my claims and some I have further info to stand firm in most of what I threw out there and with what I share either you being a professor or a simple underclassman non funded researcher such as myself you just may reconsider your thoughts , theories , and claims.

We all must be humble in our search , Not to be so proud of what we may learn from one younger or less educated as one who may have a degree for it is the one's like me who only has a High School Diploma Self funded who dedicates a great deal of my own time in the field boots on the ground Exploring and Researching for Answers. Ladies and Gentlemen Bigfooting is not a race to see who can come up with the best evidence or The Big Breaking News Discovery.

Lets Explore with our minds and open up new possibility as I take you in the points and views of my research and studies as well as the answers I am standing by till this day.

Prepare yourself to read my thoughts, my research, my reasons behind my belief and draw your own conclusion on what are the real facts verses speculation in the Bigfoot Community.

Bigfoot Vision

Who is Seeing the Mysterious undiscovered Creature ? Where are they Seeing them ?

Well we are going to do what I like to call salting the wounds of so called researchers and share some information on legit sane individual verses those who we question not just to doubt but their insanity.

Many photos and even videos that flood social media portraying the Bigfoot creature that many of us do find exciting with hopes of relief towards our belief in such a being, Then on the other hand you have images of Dark distorted forestry , smudged up images with glares or even images of tree stumps or a simple spec in the blurry distance; the sad truth is people find these abominations as truth and get such a sickening praise or recognition over all this.

Ladies and Gentlemen of the Jury let it be known this pollution is destroying the credibility of many who strive to put forth the truth with logic. There is a great deception among us here and I will share what is going on here , but I ask you to brace yourselves for the answer to why this is happening.

First of all let me introduce *Parodoilia* a simple illusion of what the mind is projecting causing deception of an image that is not present nor is it real. Ok this subject has been much debated over several occasions on various photos and has gotten to the point where the ones who argue against it to defend their lie of deception has altered the truth behind the meaning of this psychological phenomenon. Well there is two points or possibility here that is happening with this and it can only be one or the other. One there is a lie that has been told one to many times and the one sharing it has fallen into their own deceit so deep that they came to the point of believing it themselves, This does happen often.

The people who fall under this way of believing are also called or referred to as Neurotic People. Let me share an example here: If you see faces in random objects, you might be kind of Neurotic. That's what one new study suggests. As reported on Brain Decoder, a researcher at the NNT

Communication Science Laboratory in Tokyo gave 166 undergraduates two standard psychological tests that assess the 'big five' personality traits and emotional mood. They then showed each of the participants the same pattern of random dots and asked them to report and draw whatever shapes they saw in the dots.

Those who scored higher for Neuroticism on the psychological tests were more likely to see faces in the dots, as well as seeing plants and animals.

So do you see where I am coming from and the simple point that I'm trying to lay out here for you?

There is a serious complication here with many in the Bigfoot community, Many will not wake up from their Delusion that haunts their emotions that controls their mentality and lost way of thinking.

Why am I sharing this information? Well people we need to put our foot down but with encouragement and most of all if all possible we need to ignore this all over and I know personally that is not always avoided, I get presented with images all the time, and I do share my honest opinion but not all understand.

Some of us are so involved with our passion in this field that we become deceived into believing the utmost illogical possibilities and it drives us into a blind state of seeing the real truth. I have often had to put myself in check over many of my findings only because from the beginning of my research I had influences that I later found out and discovered that I was questioning their credibility and source of information , only to find out it had nothing to support it but was only made up just to please their own fantasy. I wanted answers for myself , So I further educated myself with science , nature , wildlife , and the ecology around me. I focused myself on the known to study the patterns and behaviors.

Have you ever asked yourselves " How can I learn or know and understand an unknown without knowing what already is known and acknowledged by science" before Seeking a Cryptid species ?
.

Stop and analyze where you are and what you are doing , There is so much hidden natural truth to see in front of you if only you can understand natural life as it stands and you can simply rule out all the obvious known species and all natural occurrences, By doing so you are moving all obstacles that are obstructing your view of what has been hidden among you.

WHO IS RELIABLE ?

This is a great and very important question we need to ask ourselves, and not take others word or say so over it. We all need to check ourselves before judging others credibility. More importantly we need to ask ourselves what is substantial evidence when it comes to Bigfoot ? Secondly Is it out there to be found , and Do we have it ? These are really tough questions that I'm asking , for one they especially apply to me , Two they need to be carefully thought over before being answered . Lets begin with Eye witnesses , but where to start.

I can share this much that I personally have had the privilege of Interviewing several former non believers of Bigfoot who never in their wildest dreams never once imagined not ever seeing a Bigfoot Actually had the impossible happen to them . These people had an eye opening occurrence and a life changer. To hear the shock and excitement in their voice combined by fear while they speak of what should of never happened to them opens up a new reality in their life.

Police officers have shared encounters with me , Hunters have experienced unexplained occurrences and events, Photo evidence has been shared to me by Hunters and Hikers of Tracks larger than any Human known to exist today and not belonging to any known animal in the forests around us. This alone does not include the many other reports taken from other researchers from around the world and the documentation and history by native Americans dating back hundreds of years and earlier of a large hairy bipedal beast roaming the forests of our own homeland.

Sadly but true according to many skeptics and more by non believers its all one big misidentification or even a Hoax. Very few of us such as myself study and researches the known wildlife commonly known and acknowledged by all scientist in order to learn and understand patterns , behaviors , sounds, and tracks in motion, and the also the diets of all living creatures, Not to mention the study of damage made from weather. By doing so this will help in serious way of distinguishing the differences apart from an unknowns construction to a piece of evidence left behind.

These researchers who study wildlife with passion who also provide

Evidence of the unknown are one's I highly recommend paying special attention to, You just may Learn the Truth.

ECBRO evidence collected

ECBRO track cluster powered to show pattern

ECBRO 22" track found 2016

Destroying the Bigfoot Community

Many of us observe and see the large number of forums surrounding and flooding social media and how so many people want praise for every little post or photo of what they are calling Bigfoot evidence, well one important problem is they fail to provide is an actual photo of a subject appearing in the photo. Sounds very familiar right ? Posting photo's with captions saying such things as *"look at the two watching me here"*

The following is an example of what hoaxers deliberately do and insist on telling the world that this is providing real Bigfoot evidence.

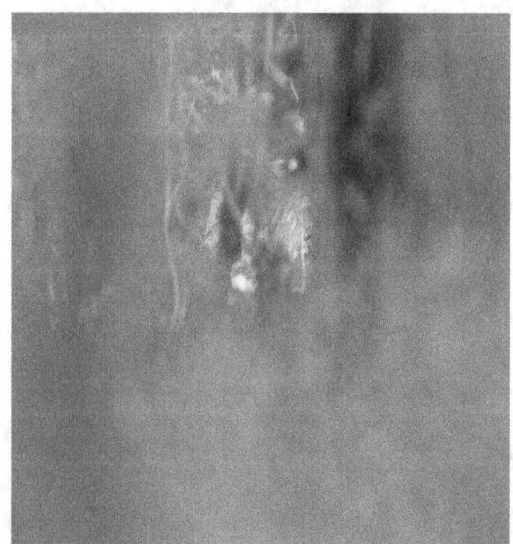

Above photo is Credited to a Hoaxer

This is the very pollution that is hurting the credibility of the ones trying to provide serious pieces of evidence to be considered towards the existence and awareness of Sasquatch. I will take you deeper into further pollution and the muck that is being thrown out there among us, so put on your hip weighters and hold on because this crap gets deep.

INTERDIMENTIONAL SCI-FI (fiction based Theory)

Why do Many believe that Bigfoot have special abilities .
Such as cloaking , telepathic powers etc. Lets keep it simple shall we.

First off Let me start off by saying all Living creatures are as organic as mankind are. We are all flesh and blood beings. We have intelligence some more than others . Humans or mankind have wild imaginations and fantasies developed from our own self conscience that are implanted into the minds so strong that we dwell on them and without doubt we believe such nonsense as a Truth.

Secondly Many animals are naturally well hidden in their environment . Many of them naturally blend with the trees of the forest & even the leaf litter of the woods.
Its all a natural ordinary happening.

No animal has powers ! Anyone who claims their own beliefs to be facts when it comes to the knowledge of Bigfoot is sadly mistaken . WHY?
Because there is no proof or evidence to back theories up.
One may swear to a continuing occurrence of sightings , but Why is it not so to others who dwell in that area ?
The Bigfoot Community has way to many attention seekers trying their darnest to gain popularity and awareness . Its sad but they do get it , but what's upsetting and yet aggravating is that many follow and believe such nonsense .
Now some on the other hand may simply be misidentified sightings of a known species such as bear or a person in hunting camo / gear.
Research is to learn & know the Organic truth not create it in a falsified way.
Step outside your fantasies and look with the naked eye. OBSERVE ,

LISTEN & THEN ANALYZE, DONT EVER "ASS"UME , that's common with many in the Bigfoot world today. Even veterinarians that don't conduct DNA studies correctly or completely take unfinished results assume before the sequence is fully compared and or finished properly do this, Causing a large following of uneducated individuals into a deception of error.

So do your homework, research out of the field, know your field of study, read and apply.

Why do so many claim theories as fact?

The truth behind Theories are they are only ideas of the human imagination, some more than others are more likely to have a chance of standing as being true.

BUT .... With out evidence to support an idea ; We as a whole can not claim theories to be true by any means.
(Research must be conducted)
BIGFOOT .... In the world we live in that has so vast of large uncharted forests all throughout our world we as enthusiast and or Researchers that have a stable mental mind do not see Bigfoot on a normal bases or we are fortunate to even see the creature at least once in our life time.
Some on the other hand have an over active imagination of seeing what they want to .
CLOAKING, PORTALS, DIMENSIONS:
There is a great explanation for these claims and theories that flood our Bigfoot community.
Science that is not understood , and education or awareness of our own living species living in their own environment, and how they are made and or adapted to live with natural elusive abilities.
A deer or a bear are great examples of blending in the forest, these

animals can disappear with simple movement behind the foliage that surround them.

Primates in their own world are great and masters of hide n go seek.

EXAMPLE – Primatologist who spend their time in the jungles and forests observing the variety of our known primate species acknowledge the simple elusive disappearing act that they do when moved into the foliage that surrounds them in their environment.

(Even within a few feet away)

So without getting to deep into further explanation be sure you consider, nature, science, and reality.

Do not rule the obvious, know the truth.

(Reference to this information found from **www.ecbro.wordpress.com**)

Unfortunately reality does not exist for these Hoaxers of the Bigfoot Community as they create a non existent world apart from the one most of us live in. There is a inter dimensional world belonging to the minds of such people a Sci-fi world that is pure fictional , and this is used and taught in order for their unexplained to exist. Bigfoot is believed to pass to and from one realm to another , and even having the abilities to disappear from anyone who may encounter them at will. These people are pure illogical , Never having evidence to support any such possibility of this non sense. This sort of thing really hurts many of us because we are looked at as not being normal or some having a coo-coo sanity, a mental illness as one may refer to it as, but How can we fix this ? Simple we need to start shunning the one's putting it out there, Not giving the attention they seek.

One theory in particular that is very common in the Bigfoot Community that effects the credibility and the sincerity of most of us serious Researchers is the subject of *Cloaking* , What is is this referring to ?

 This is the ability to be able to turn invisible according to many who can only provide irrational answers.

So lets look at the meaning behind this:

Invisibility is the state of an object that cannot be <u>seen</u>. An object in this state is said to be invisible (literally, "not visible"). The term is often used in *fantasy*/*science fiction*, *where objects cannot be seen by* magical *or* technological *means; however, its effects can also be demonstrated in the real world, particularly in* physics *and perceptual* psychology *classes.*

Since objects can be seen by light in the visible spectrum *from a source reflecting off their surfaces and hitting the viewer's* **eye***, the most natural form of invisibility (whether real or fictional) is an object that neither reflects nor absorbs light (that is, it allows light to pass through it). This is known as* **transparency***, and is seen in many naturally occurring materials (although no naturally occurring material is 100% transparent).*

Invisibility perception depends on several optical and visual factors. **F***or example, invisibility depends on the* **eyes** *of the observer and/or the instruments used. Thus an object can be classified as "invisible to" a person, animal, instrument, etc. In research on censorial* **perception** *it has been shown that invisibility is perceived in cycles.*

Invisibility is often considered to be the supreme form of **camouflage***, as it does not reveal to the viewer any kind of* **vital signs***,* **visual** *effects, or any frequencies of the electromagnetic* **spectrum** *detectable to the human eye, instead making use of* **radio***,* **infrared** *or* **ultraviolet** *wavelengths.*

In **illusion optics***, invisibility is a special case of illusion effects: the illusion of free space.*

CLOAKING is not a magical trick or power belonging to any living creature or being on earth. This is one of two forms of logically explained camouflage.

A – An animal of the earth is in its own natural habitat and environment state of living and can naturally blend in with its surroundings and not to mention that some rare species may have what is known as translucent hair or fur allowing for a natural blend, Translucent allows lights to pass through an object.

B – A person(s) using a form of clothing to disguise themselves within a habitat not if their own living quarters and/or the use of modern technology normally associated with military gear to reflect it's surroundings causing the illusion of invisibility.

Let it be known that Science is far come to the existence and has many explanations yet to establish truth with the many theories it studies. Science is often wrong but yet also has proven logical happenings over and over regarding natural occurrences. NOT MAGICAL POWERS THAT DO NOT EXIST.

BE LOGICAL, BE WISE , BE SANE , AND ANALYZE BEFORE YOU STATE YOUR THOUGHTS AND OPINIONS, HAVE INFORMATION THAT SUPPORTS YOUR CONCLUSIONS. (Reference to this information found from **www.ecbro.wordpress.com**)

BIGFOOT
THE
BEGINING

We are going to touch base on a very touchy and not so agreeable subject here. Again who said Science has all the answers ?

If Evolution was a firm guide to the origins of all mankind summed up as a tree of life consisting of many branches to every form of Primate both human & non human then why are branches either missing or producing nothing ? The tree has become a Theory or guessing plant rather than anything such productive as far as providing answers ; instead it has produced more contradictions than Substantive results.

Lets keep our focus on our Big Hairy Friend Bigfoot here. I have often stated my belief with Bigfoot having a close relation or connection to the Once existing *Gigantopithecus . Who or What was this massive beast ?*

Gigantopithecus (from the Ancient Greek γίγας *gigas* "giant", and πίθηκος *pithekos* "ape") is an extinct __genus__ of __ape__ that existed from perhaps nine million years to as recently as one hundred thousand years ago,__[1]__ in what is now China, India, and Vietnam, placing *Gigantopithecus* in the same time frame and geographical location as several __homini__ species.__[2]__ The __fossil record__ suggests that individuals of the species *Gigantopithecus blacki* were the largest known apes that ever lived, standing up to 3 m (9.8ft), and weighing up to 540 kg (1,190lb)

Lets take a look at what popular theory has to say when it comes to relating or comparing Bigfoot with Gigantopithecus Blacki :

- *Some Bigfoot hunters say Gigantopithecus is alive and well, hiding out in the forests of the Pacific Northwest. Other Sasquatch enthusiasts, however, point out this is unlikely, as Bigfoot is reported to be a swift, agile, upright walker—not a lumbering, 1,200-pound quadruped.*

HOWEVER

- *Some Professors do agree with the point of this species not being related giving the limited data that is available.*
- *One theory shared for this to be impossible is that Giganto was not upright .*

Now we need to look at the Evolutionary Theory and what does it suggest when it comes to the origins of mankind.

- Man was not an upright being . Over a period of time developed and adapted into an upright formation.
- Man was considered to be classified as a great ape of the earlier stages of adaptation or development prior to what we are today.
- Now Man Vs Gigantopithecus …. Why did only one become upright ? Why did Early Ape become Man ? Do you see the Contradiction that I am trying to expose ?
- So here is where and why I am standing on the possibility that Bigfoot is associated and related to Gigantopithecus Blacki and I don't even agree or believe with evolution, but If man is capable of becoming upright , Why not G.blacki ? Is it so hard to believe such a thing and keep bigfoot all in its own classified section of being a species all of it's own kind, and having different forms or sub species depending on the various regions.

Something to seriously think about and really consider

Non Human Primates Compared to Bigfoot

What do you really know when it comes to Our known Non human Primates and the behaviors, and communication with each other ?

Lets get familiar with the basics of our Non human Primates and try to understand them.

Non-Human Primate Communication

Odors, **vocalizations**, gestures, and facial expressions are used by non-human primates to inform others of their psychological state and present concerns, which is an important clue to what they are likely to do next. In the picture on the left, the outstretched hand and pleading facial expression directed toward another group member are obvious indications of this chimpanzee's appeal for sharing. It also probably reflects and reinforces his or her lower position on the dominance hierarchy within the community. Primatologists have observed that some communication patterns are commonly used by many primate species. These are discussed below.

Prosimians have excellent _olfactory_ sensing abilities. It is not surprising, therefore, that they usually use body odors to communicate. Adult male ring-tailed lemurs regularly mark their woodland territories with chemicals produced by scent glands in their wrists. This is similar to dogs, wolves, and cats marking their territories with urine. In both cases, the scent is recognized as a personal signature. Tamarins and marmosets also use scented urine to mark the gum trees that are important food sources in their territories. In all of these species, **scent marking** is a way of claiming territory and warning off intruders.

Using scent to communicate is not unique to prosimians. All primates, including humans, do so to some extent. People do not mark territory with scent or battle each other with it, but we do produce odors that may attract or repulse others. Think about the effect you might have on your friends if you did not bathe or shower for several days. Humans have learned to cover up body odors with perfumes and other products. Our cultures tell us that some of these odors are attractive. However, our bodies also produce pheromones, which are chemicals that give off powerful, often subliminal, odors that have effects on the physiology and behavior of others in our species whether they are aware of it or not. Very importantly, there are different male and female pheromones that play a part in sexual attraction and ovulation regulation. It is likely that all primates produce such pheromones.

Q. When researching out in the field do you ever experience a higher volume of activity when you are accompanied by a female ?

* This has been reported in many cases, especially experiencing close vocalizations, and/or Tree knocks.

Cont'd

Most primate species, including humans, use threatening gestures, stares, and poses to intimidate others. Primatologists refer to this particular use of body language as **agonistic displays** .

Among non-human primates, they are usually sufficient to prevent physical fighting. In fact, physically violent encounters are rare among them. The dominant male in a monkey or ape community can usually prevent major conflicts and keep order by the use of often subtle agonistic displays. For instance, male baboons flash their eyelids when they are angry and want to intimidate others. If this isn't sufficient in its effect, they open their mouths widely in a manner that looks like human yawning. This is usually the last warning before attacking. Since the marmosets and tamarins cannot significantly change their facial expressions, their agonistic displays are different. Adult males chirp repeatedly and turn around to show their genitals from behind. This is the ultimate threat for them.

Most primate species communicate affection and reduce group tension by what are known as affiliative behaviors. These include calmly sitting close to each other, touching, and mutually grooming. The latter is referred to as **allogrooming** in contrast to self or autogrooming.

Allogrooming is a powerful tool for communication. It is used by both monkeys and apes to reinforce male-female mate bonds as well as same sex friendship bonds. Chimpanzees often have ecstatic bouts of allogrooming that go on for hours when an old acquaintance rejoins the community. They also do it to calm emotions following wild, aggressive outbursts by angry adult males. Most members of the community also seem to very much enjoy grooming infants and may compete for the opportunity. Allogrooming usually has measurable physiological effects on both the individual being groomed and the one doing the grooming. It can cause the release of endorphin's into the blood. These are hormones that have opiate-like effects on the body--they reduce the sensation of pain and cause a pleasant emotional state.

It is clear that allogrooming results in both social and psychological benefits for non-human primates. It often serves much the same purposes for humans, whether it be in the private setting of a family at home, where a parent might brush a child's hair, or in a public barbershop or beauty salon. The experience of having someone run their fingers through your hair and massage your head in the process is usually physically pleasurable, and it generally provides a period of time removed from work or school concerns when relaxed, casual conversation occurs.

Among some species of primates, including humans, the urge to allogroom is so strong as to result in grooming animals of other species. Among non-human primates, inter-species allogrooming sometimes occurs when they are in captivity and deprived of the opportunity to groom their own kind. They are even known to groom people. However, it does not seem to be a pattern of wild non-human primates.

PRIMATE KNOWLEDGE

CONTINUES

LOCOMOTION Chimpanzees usually walk using all fours (on the soles of their feet ,They can walk upright (when they need to use their arms to reach or defend.. Chimps are also very acrobatic & good at climbing trees, They can swing from branch to branch.

LIFE SPAN Chimpanzees live about 60 years in captivity; (like most animals, they live much longer in captivity)

HABITAT Chimpanzees live in a wide variety of habitats, including rock ledges and clearings), woodlands, swamp forests, and grass lands.

DISTRIBUTION The different subspecies of chimpanzees live in different parts of western and central Africa in 21 different countries, from the Atlantic coast to well inland.

Chimpanzee populations are becoming increasingly fragmented as parts of their habitat are used by people.

REPRODUCTION AND BABY CHIMPANZEES Chimpanzees are fully grown and able to reproduce at 12-1 are pregnant for about 8.5-9 months.

Female chimpanzees carefully nurture their young. Babies stay on the mother's back at about 6 months. After that they remain with their mother for about 7 years.

POPULATION COUNTS Chimpanzee populations are decreasing; they are threaten numbers are disputed. Estimates range from 100,000 to 20

JANE GOODALL Jane Goodall is a scientist who spent most of her adult life in Gombe National Park, Tanzania (it was then the Gombe Tanganyika), Africa. Her field-work, which lasted for almost given us a tremendous amount of information about these very similar to that of humans.

THE EVOLUTION OF CHIMPANZEES The earliest-known primates date from about 70 million & greater apes (family Pongidae, gorillas, chimpanzees, bono the lesser apes (family Hylobatidae, gibbons and siamangs)

And According to scientists they believe in theory how they are part of us although I stand apart from the Evolutionary theory when it comes to man & ape.

SCIENTISTS SAY:
The chimpanzee is the animal that is closest to people gene & very similar DNA (about 98% of human and chimpanzee share a common ancestor.

NO I DO NOT BELIEVE THIS ALTHOUGH DNA MAY BE SIMILAR WE ARE NOT THE SAME NOR DID WE COME FROM THE SAME.

With having. the basic understanding of chimps ; Have you.properly observed & done the right research to see these similarities in our own back yard?
Have you seen all the signs that indicate and point at Bigfoot being a primate ?
(IF NOT)

WELL START PAYING ATTENTION !

CLASSIFICATION Chimpanzees belong to the:

Kingdom Animalia (all animals) Phylum Chordata Subphylum Vertebrata (animals with backbones) Class Mammalia (warm-blooded animals with fur and Order Primates (which is comprised of 11 families, in marmosets, lesser apes, great apes, and humans) Family Pongidae (the great apes, including gorillas, ch orangutans) Genus Pan (chimpanzees and bonobos) Species troglodytes - the Chimpanzee Subspecies P. t. verus - the western subspe some small populations in Guinea, Sierra Le Subspecies P. t. troglodytes - the central su also from eastern Nigeria to the Ubanghi Riv Subspecies P. t. schweinfurthi - the eastern (found from southern Lake Tanganyika in Ta to Burundi, Rwanda, Uganda and southern S Species paniscus - the Bonobo or pygmy chimp.

- How is the behavior and communication of our known non primates any different from what we all observe through our own research and explorations ?

- How well do you Observe and pay attention to the unknown sounds , the tree knocks ,and the various formations found that we can rule out from weather ?

- Q. Are all these occurrences really unknown ?

- A. No they are not ; they do belong and relate to our known non human primates.

- Ok are you confused in what I may be getting at ? You must be thinking that I am stating that Bigfoot is one of Our known Non Human primates. The answer to that is No I am not saying that at all.

- What is Bigfoot ? My honest opinion I'll share is this, that He is a Form of Non human primate related to the Great ape family but a species all in itself. A distant relative to the great Gigantopithecus who is believed to be completely extinct.

What I am trying to do here is to set your minds apart from what society has programmed into you , we were giving the basic tools designed to have us all think and develop our way of thinking to stay clear of the real truth. We really need to open our minds up and think outside the box of man's theories. Am I saying all that I have in this book is the one true answer, No but Research and continuous results have led me here. I have made many errors and mistakes and I have found correction the deeper I searched.

BIGFOOT POPULATION

Is the east coast underestimated when it comes to Bigfoot population?

I believe it is but that's my two cents.

What's so different on the West compared to the East ?

* Is it the dense vast forest?
* Bigger mountains?
* Or the rain fall?
* Is it abundance of food selection?

OK all these do matter, but although the West may provide these in a larger amount or quantity, The East has all the same sources and a slight vastness of forest.

Researchers on the East Coast strive to provide evidence as well as answers to the community, as we put forth effort, time, and funds out of our own pockets.
Field Research, Observations, Scientific studies, but with sane logical truth with out overdoing theories that have no solid ground of evidence.
Daniel J. Benoit is the founder of the East Coast Bigfoot Researchers Organization and along with other team members have gone forth almost on a daily bases to seek out evidence and truth to bring home to you, to lay the pieces of the puzzle out to provide the right answers.
Evidence from various East Coast Bigfoot groups and Teams have been shared openly.

I work and compare studies, and other findings with fellow friends and researchers.

Bigfoot History

Various locations up and down the East coast for 100+ years have been reported. Tracing back to our Own Native Americans whom document all forest dwellers.

Where did they come from?

Well lets all think of this: **The Bering land bridge is only theory, however Bigfoot/Sasquatch like creatures have held native American legend history as long as most really know if not longer. Is it impossible to believe that they were actually Native here among the various native tribes as well??? There is fossil record of other known primates once existing here in the US.**

Even Canada has records, Alaska has even had Evidence of Tropical plants such as palm trees indicating a warmer climate at one point in time, So I believe in the possibility of them already being here or migrating from up north.

QUESTION & ANSWER

- Q. If there are so many Bigfoot in Just U.S. Alone well where do they hide ?

- A. Well for one where we don't venture into , a few possible place(s) are hidden caves , heavy clusters of down fallen timber on High Ridges deep in the forest.

- Q. Do you they stay in one place for living ?

- A. No they move around from place to place and cover a lot of terrain to seek out food and other shelter. This also allows for safety and protection.

- Q. Do they mark their Territories ?

- A. Yes I believe so, Many formations not made naturally from weather have been found some of these markers do relate similar to native American styles , but a great majority of them do have similarities to what our known primates create.

- Q. Do they hunt in groups ?

- A. Yes I do believe they do work as a unit , such as our known Primates do. From observations from encounters I have taken notice that deer were always present, however I also believe that they do occasionally hunt independently at times.

WILDLIFE AWARENESS

Lets get some knowledge on one particular mammal that I also compare to Bigfoot for various reasons; The north American black bear.

This monster of the forest is often mistaken as a Bigfoot for the Large dark appearance , and for those not familiar or knowledgeable with their Track pattern it too can create a great deal of confusion. They almost have a human like track pattern or identity but do not be fooled.

Here is some great information and facts you should know:

BLACK BEARS FACTS

A touch from legend to facts of the American black bear.

Cont'd

Black bears feature prominently in the stories of some of America's indigenous peoples. One tale tells of how the black bear was a creation of the Great Spirit, while the grizzly was created by the Evil Spirit. In the mythology of the Haida, Tlingit,Tsimshian people of the Northwest Coast, mankind first learned to respect bears when a girl married the son of black bear Chieftain. In Kwakiutl mythology, black and brown bears became enemies when Grizzly Bear Woman killed Black Bear Woman for being lazy. Black Bear Woman's children, in turn, killed Grizzly Bear Woman's own cubs. The Navajo believed that the Big Black Bear was chief among the bears of the four directions surrounding Sun's house, and would pray to it in order to be granted its protection during raids.

Morris Michtom, the creator of the teddy bear, was inspired to make the toy when he came across a cartoon of Theodore Roosevelt refusing to shoot a black bear cub tied to a tree was named after Winnipeg, a female black bear cub that lived at London Zoo from 1915 until her death in 1934. A black bear cub who in the spring of 1950 was caught in the Capitan Gap fire was made into the living representative of Smokey Bear, the mascot of the United States Forest Service.

The American black bear is the mascot of The University of Maine and Baylor University, where the university houses two live black bears on campus.

Sleeping Bear Dunes is named after a Native American legend, where a female bear and her cub swam across Lake Michigan. Exhausted from their journey, the bears rested on the shoreline and fell sound asleep. Over the years, the sand covered them up, creating a huge sand dune.

Attacks on humans

Although an adult bear is quite capable of killing a human, American black bears typically avoid confronting humans when possible. Unlike grizzly bears, which became a subject of fearsome legend among the European settlers of North America, black bears were rarely considered overly dangerous, even though they lived in areas where the pioneers had settled. Black bears rarely attack when confronted by humans, and usually limit themselves to making mock charges, emitting blowing noises and swatting the ground with their fore paws. The number of black bear attacks on humans is higher than those of the brown bear in North America, though this is largely because the black species considerably outnumbers the brown rather than greater aggressiveness.

The incidence of bear attacks in parks and campgrounds declined after the introduction of bear-resistant garbage cans and other reforms

Compared to brown bear attacks, aggressive encounters with black bears rarely lead to serious injury. However, the majority of black bear attacks tend to be motivated by hunger rather than territoriality, and thus victims have a higher probability of surviving by fighting back rather than submitting. Unlike grizzlies, female black bears do not display the same level of protectiveness to their cubs, and seldom attack humans in their vicinity. However, occasionally, attacks by protective mothers do occur. The worst recorded fatality incident occurred in May 1978, in which a black bear killed three teenagers who were fishing in Algonquin Park in Canada Another exceptional, spree-like attack occurred in August 1997 in Liard River Hot Springs Provincial Park in Canada, when an emaciated black bear attacked a child and mother, killing the mother as well as an adult man who tried to intervene. This bear was shot while mauling a fourth victim.

The majority of attacks happened in national parks, usually near campgrounds, where the bears had become habituated to close human proximity and food conditioned. Out of 1,028 incidents of black bears acting aggressively toward people, 107 resulted in injury, were recorded from 1964 to 1976 in the Great Smoky Mountains National Park, and occurred mainly in tourist hot spots where people regularly fed the bears handouts. In almost every case where open dumps or handouts that had previously attracted black bears were ceased, the amount of aggressive encounters with bears have decreased precipitously over time However, in the before mentioned case of the spree attack in Liard River Hot Springs, the attacking bear was believed to have been previously almost fully dependent on a local garbage dump that had closed and was starving as a result of the loss of that food source. Attempts to relocate bears are typically unsuccessful, as black bears seem to be able to return to their home range even without familiar landscape cues.

On October 27, 2009, Canadian wildlife experts and managers for Cape Breton Highlands National Park thought Taylor Mitchell's suspect of her predatory attack on the Skyline Trail was a black bear at first, but they soon realized it was a pack of coyotes.

Livestock and crop predation

A limitation of food sources in early spring and wild berry and nut crop failures during summer months may be contributing factors to black bears regularly feeding from commercial human-based food sources. Crops are frequently eaten by these bears, especially during autumn hyperphagia when natural foods are scarce. Favored crops may include apples, oats and corns. Black bears can do extensive damage in some areas of the northwestern United States by stripping the bark from trees and feeding on the cambium. Livestock depredations by black bears occur mostly in spring. Though black bears have the capacity to (and occasionally do) hunt adult cattle and horses, they seem to prefer smaller, more easily overwhelmed prey such as sheep, goats, calves, and pigs. They normally kill by biting the neck and shoulders, though they may break the neck or back of prey with blows from the paws. Evidence of a bear attack includes claw marks and is frequently found on the neck, back, and shoulders of larger animals. Surplus killing of sheep and goats are common. Bears have been known to frighten livestock herds over cliffs, causing injuries and death to many animals; whether or not this is intentional is not known. Occasionally, pets, especially dogs, which are most prone to harass a bear, are killed by black bears. It is not recommended to use unleashed dogs as a deterrent from bear attacks. Although large, aggressive dogs sometimes cause a bear to run, if pressed, angry bears frequently turn the tables and end up chasing the dog in return. A bear in pursuit of a pet dog has the potential to threaten both canid and human lives.

Bear awareness in towns

In an effort to help prevent conflicts with bears, many towns in British Columbia developed bear aware programs. The main premise of these programs is to teach humans to manage foods that attract bears. Keeping garbage securely stored, harvesting fruit when ripe, securing livestock behind electric fences, and storing pet food indoors are all measures promoted by bear aware programs. Revelstoke, British Columbia is a community that demonstrates the success of this approach. Before the community had an education program, an average of 27 bears were killed in Revelstoke each year; after the program began, the average mortality has dropped to just 7 bears per year.

Black Bear Tracks:

Often mistaken as humanoid tracks.

Some Cryptid researchers lacking proper awareness are quick to assume false conclusions toward the identity of bear tracks believing them to be the mysterious Bigfoot or Sasquatch.

Guess again my friend. Learn your known wildlife before seeking the unknown.

realist
E.C.B.R.O.
A TEAM who believes in facts to determine truth. Either deeply **Objective** or extremely **Subjective**.

STRUCTURES
AND
FORMATIONS

The following are believed to be not natural but created on purpose for a particular reason:

TRACKS

The following are a few tracks found by the ECBRO research program
(ECBRO DISCOVERY PROJECT)

DEBUNKING
&
RULING OUT

 One of the biggest neglects in the Bigfoot Community among Researchers today and it has grown to become out of hand.

This is not a difficult task or procedure but it is where logic can be revealed and Science is used, Most importantly "common sense" So Let us start with photo evidence , the following questions refer to the tools we need .

- How familiar are you with the landscape ? Example do you know layout of the trees, and falling timber and yes the stumps in the area?

- How familiar are you with your own device ?

- Did you do take a follow up photo of the same exact location with the same landscape? This is highly recommended and needed for comparison purposes. This will also shed some light on if there really was a subject/being in your original photo.

- Ask yourselves and follow the above for improvement on your photography.

Next lets talk about vocalizations, many of us record and document various vocals from our area of focus and at times we pick up sounds unfamiliar to our knowledge or our own built in data base aka our brain. On big problem I've observed with online posts are people are quick to assume or either falsely judge a piece of evidence. Some have simply embarrassed themselves by posting an obvious known sound, but research and doing your own homework could of saved you all that trouble. I can't stress enough how importantly it is to study all known wildlife in all aspects involved. In following sections I touch base more with the known wildlife.

Many outdoors man claim to have full knowledge or sense with the outdoors but throughout observations they lack much awareness .

I can't stress enough about one common Animal in North America and again it is the Black Bear . This is one Wild Animal I really recommend getting very familiar with. They share a very similar way of life next to a Bigfoot. I have personally found this throughout my research. Lets recap and read more about black bears. Awareness is really needed.

BASIC FACTS ABOUT BLACK BEARS

The American black bear is the smallest of the three bears species found in North America, and are found only in North America. Black bears have short, non-retractable claws that give them an excellent tree-climbing ability.

Black bear fur is usually a uniform color except for a brown muzzle and light markings that sometimes appear on their chests. Eastern populations are usually black in color while western populations often show brown, cinnamon, and blond coloration in addition to black. Black bears with white-bluish fur are known as Kermode (glacier) bears and these unique color phases are only found in coastal British Columbia, Canada.

Diet

American black bears are omnivorous: plants, fruits, nuts, insects, honey, salmon, small mammals and carrion. In northern regions, they eat spawning salmon. Black bears will also occasionally kill young deer or moose calves.

Population

It is estimated that there are at least 600,000 black bears in North America. In the United States, there are estimated to be over 300,000 individuals. However, the Louisiana black bear (Ursus americanus luteolu) and Florida black bear (Ursus americanus floridanus) are unique subspecies with small populations. The Louisiana black bear is federally listed as a threatened species and the Florida black bear is estimated to number 3,000.

Range

The American black bear is distributed throughout North America, from Canada to Mexico and in at least 40 states in the U.S. They historically occupied nearly all of the forested regions of North America, but in the U.S. they are now restricted to the forested areas less densely occupied by humans. In Canada, black bears still inhabit most of their historic range except for the intensively farmed areas of the central plains. In Mexico, black bears were thought to have inhabited the mountainous regions of the northern states but are now limited to a few remnant populations.

Behavior

Black bears are extremely adaptable and show a great variation in habitat types, though they are primarily found in forested areas with thick ground vegetation and an abundance of fruits, nuts, and vegetation. In the northern areas, they can be found in the tundra, and they will sometimes forage in fields or meadows.

Black bears tend to be solitary animals, with the exception of mothers and cubs. The bears usually forage alone, but will tolerate each other and forage in groups if there is an abundance of food in one area.

Most black bears hibernate depending on local weather conditions and availability of food during the winter months. In regions where there is a consistent food supply and warmer weather throughout the winter, bears may not hibernate at all or do so for a very brief time. Females give birth and usually remain denned throughout the winter, but males and females without young may leave their dens from time to time during winter months.

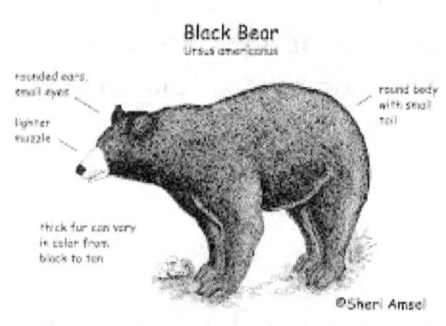

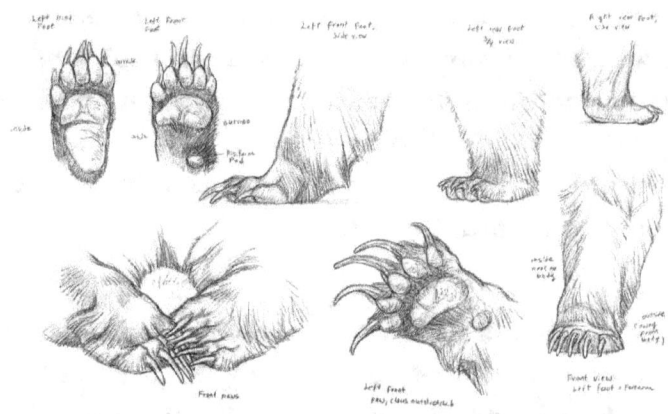

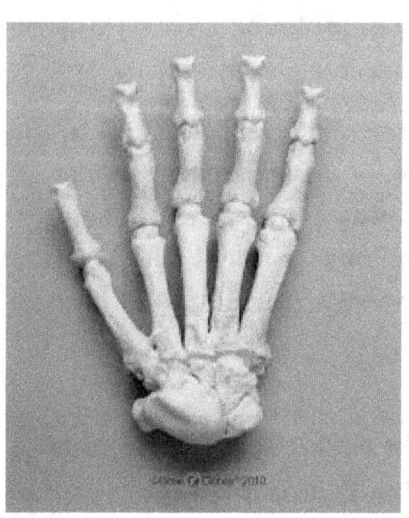

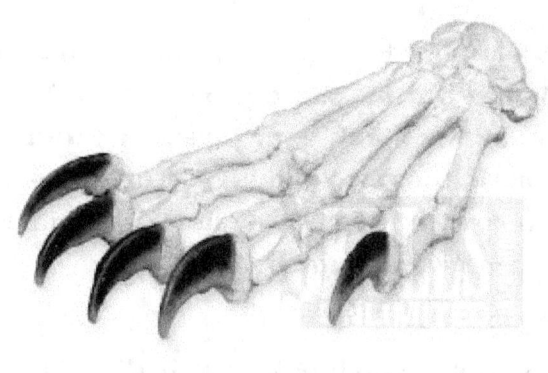

WHO OR WHAT ARE SOME PEOPLE SAYING BIGFOOT IS ?

I believe that Sasquatch are flesh and blood, a very unique primate with an awesome look (why) I have come to this belief through my own observation.

Donna Hamrick

He is some form of Large demon with Red evil looking eyes , That I wish on no one to ever encounter.

Gary Johnson Sr.

A Big Hairy Ape

Shakey Junior

Something that used to peek in the windows when I lived in New York. A very elusive but curious creature.

Claire Furber

After seeing what I seen during my encounter I can say it is more human than primate . Just in the facial features and the way it done the way I did . Really thought I was a goner but now I see it other than a primate . Flesh and blood for Sure the Lord only knows.

Tracy Arnold

North American unknown primate

Mark Hamblen

"A lot of Theories contradict themselves
Explain please
Like when people say that their human, but they show primate habits. Then people say they're primates yet they have human level intelligence. Then they say its a human/primate cross breed which is impossible."

Zach Starrick

A primate that was here long before or around the time periods of the paleo people in north America. The paleo people are not to be confused with modern native Americans who shares absolutely no decent from the north American paleo Indians. This to me also explains why the northern Russian Bigfoot most closely resembles the north American Bigfoot more than any other so called Bigfoot in other countries... They could have came from north America or Russia to the other side. We will never know this part. Just a smarter, rather very huge primate that still exists in small numbers in certain areas..

Andrew Mysinger

Well ladies and Gentleman you just read some the opinions and even Eye witnesses who have seen and experienced a sighting.

Now in my next section I will go into where I stand on my opinion and what I use that supports my belief.

The Author's opinion of Bigfoot with reason

To many reports from eye witnesses share so many but yet differences on the description of what Bigfoot is and looks like, well now we need to look at the more important details that are ignored when It comes to self classification of where we can place our Friend of the Forest in the Animal Kingdom, This is not scientific nor is it official but we need to start somewhere in order to begin with a place to search for more accurate results.

Lets start with a few key factors that will help explain where I stand on what Bigfoot is:

- Vocalizations related or equal to our Known Non Human Primates experienced in our own forest.

- Stick structures and formations found and ruled out Not from weather that was created by hands belonging to an intelligence great in strength.

- Experienced encounters with observations portraying Non Human Primate behaviors and movement.

- Large and heavy Bipedal Movement

- Fresh Trees and Limbs found twisted in a 180 up to a 360 degree position.

- Tracks found having similar details shared with our Non Human Primates.

- Dermal ridges not belonging to Humans but only to Non Human

Primates.

Cont'd

I do believe my points speak for themselves on where I am getting at here. Yes I the Author with doing my research with the results I have found throughout field work and observations that I have come to the conclusion that Bigfoot is Clearly a Non Human Primate different from our known Primates But sharing similarities of traits as well appearances based off the data shared across the world To simply be Its own Non Human Primate all in itself. Having a relation to the once known believed to be extinct Gigantopithecus .

But Stop right There , Don't throw judgment or hate on my results, I am here presenting Found data based of the Research I have conducted thus far Not having no DNA data to go by. Ladies and Gents you need to start with what you find the subject to most resemble in all factors not just appearance. If we soley went on with the assumptions on what few believe then we get nowhere. EXAMPLE If you are finding the subject to be a Primate of some form then there is your starting point, Start your research based off the behaviors and patterns of such and compare. Simple right? Yes It is do not make this into difficult science.

In the words of Shakey Junior always quoting , If it quacks like a duck then it must be a duck.

It is the same concept here. Think about it people !

A BIGFOOT RESEARCHER ?

I am not going to get into a long statement here, but only point out a few obvious but random details with questions you should ask yourself.:

* Being out in the woods all the time does not make you a researcher – One who is observant but yet takes notice of the world around them and seeing life for what it is authentically but yet simply taking it all in.

Knowing the patterns & behaviors of wildlife will teach us a lot .

All living creatures are living organisms that some go through changes based off their environmental lifestyle, climate, and so forth.

Photo Evidence:
Ask any professional photographer who does take photos of nature & wildlife – Their photos will not lie but only reveal what is truly there. Right?

If you take a photo of any living creature; Shouldn't you or anyone else for that matter be able to identify it ?

If your photos are no more than,blurry,trees, stumps & bushes do not try to convince people of what's not there.
(Example) Claiming you have a Bigfoot in the photo or anything else that is not visible to identify with out question or doubt.

If you are the only one who can see what others can not – sorry but there is nothing in it.

CONT'D

RESEARCHERS OF ANY FIELD:

What makes you a researcher ?
*What are you researching?
*Did you study the subject of interest?
*Did you read up on all affiliated topics?
*Where are you researching?
*Do you have proof that will uphold your alleged so called evidence that will authenticate the specimen to speak for itself?
Example: Do you have Evidence from where the specimen actually came from to state undoubtedly what you say it is?
My reply to this is clear; if you do not then do not say or claim until you do.

 * REALLY THINK WHAT'S SAID AND ASKED ABOVE....!

A real Researcher does not lie or hoax to gain attention or popularity .
A real Researcher provides real conclusive evidence. And does not fake it.
A real Researcher has real photos of clear images that can be undoubtedly identified.
A real field Researcher takes notes and observes nature & changes .

WHAT ARE YOU ?

ARE YOU POPULAR BECAUSE OF ALL THE PHOTOS YOU SHARE THAT YOU SAY HAS A BIGFOOT OR SOME OTHER CRYPTID IN THEM & OTHERS BELIEVE THEM TO BECAUSE YOUR SAYING SO? YOU GAINED FALSE RESPECT BECAUSE THERE ARE SO MANY GULLIBLE BIGFOOT ENTHUSIASTS OUT HERE THAT WILL BELIEVE ANYTHING YOU TELL THEM.

SOME OF MY OWN FRIENDS IN THIS COMMUNITY ARE DECEIVED AND ITS A SHAME BUT I WILL SPEAK OUT.

ABOUT THE AUTHOR

Do know where I stand !

Theories flood the world we live in, But why do so many take them as fact with out proof or evidence?

Are they that anxious or uneducated to quote and swear by them just to pretend they know something in life?

Some individuals in the world of Bigfoot teach & spread false claims or say they saw this or that but want to call it truth, but get this They do not have nothing to show for what they speak of.
Funny right? Well sadly its truth but many follow into the deception of these so called teachers or researchers.

Anyone can claim or make statements but what do they have to back it up?

Am I a know it all? Am I an expert? No not at all.....

But who exactly am I in the BIGFOOT COMMUNITY?
I am one of the few logical sane down to earth individuals among you.
I conduct research and studies both in & out of the field. I study and research many of our known wildlife.
It is crucial to know and understand what already does exists and that is acknowledged.
I compare behaviors and patterns of the known wildlife with other unnatural findings to perhaps distinguish between the various species among us in order that we may have a sense of understanding that what is found can be explained logically.
I question many and even those associated with me for the purpose of coming to an understanding. I speak bluntly to correct those who make CLAIMS as fact, I ask for evidence that upholds their claims.
I am often questioned for knowledge of those who are inquiring about the BIGFOOT TRUTH regarding various topics, and I give my educated

opinion and use my known knowledge of research studied in the field of wildlife.   Cont'd

Anyone who hunts all their life or been in the woods all their life doesn't make them a Researcher.

A Researcher is one who is willing to investigate and rule out obvious happenings and the different species that may be responsible for what is found among us.

Comparing the various signs and findings as Well as analyzing conditions of the weather and the Creation of the destruction made from natural occurrences will truly be a lesson to oneself prior to making claims.

My Mission & Goal

I am dedicated to finding the truth in everything life throws at me, I am dedicated in knowing the truth, I am and will stand my ground on my point of view and will not be a follower of others say so or claims, I will consider the many theories and research them for myself as I have always done. I will not settle for one man's teachings as my own beliefs until proven otherwise.

I will aim to teach and research logically as possible. I will be the voice of reason in the BIGFOOT COMMUNITY, I will continue to seek out other level headed and like minded people to help spread the awareness of the ECBRO® and I will make it known that we are a serious, honest, truth seeking TEAM *of real individuals who will find the answers no matter how long it takes.*

I am obligated to the BIGFOOT COMMUNITY to be who I am. Bigfoot Research is more than my passion it is my life to give only the truth as it is learned with proof.

*I need support from those who understand and who are willing to stand up for who we are dedicate themselves to truth.
*I am Daniel J. Benoit the founder of the ECBRO®
*Researcher & Mentor for those wanting to join the team.
*Host of the ECBRO DISCOVERY NEWS BLOG CAST on YouTube channel ECBRO98.
SUBSCRIBE today to follow research and LIVE PODCAST shows, check out our videos of past guests and our various open discussions.

Find us on Squatch Zone Radio – a blogtalkradio.com show And LIKE us on our ECBRO LIKE page. Join our Facebook pages.

Do you have a report to share with us ? Do you want to have your voice heard ? Then we welcome you with open arms . Contact me

ECBRO98@GMAIL.COM

VISIT

WWW.ECBRO.WORDPRESS.COM

ECBRO- East Coast Bigfoot Researchers Organization ©

AUTHOR

Daniel J. Benoit

BIGFOOT

THEORIES VS FACTS

Going Against The Grains of Science ©